Royal Homes in Gloucestershire

Geoffrey Sanders
and
David Verey

ALAN SUTTON
1981

Preface

Highgrove, Gatcombe Park and Nether Lypiatt Manor are set only a few miles apart on the south western edge of the Cotswolds. These three estates have, in recent years, firmly established Gloucestershire's links with royalty.

Royal links can be traced back to Saxon times. After the Conquest, William I made a tradition of keeping Christmas at Gloucester and held his Parliament there. It was from Gloucester in the year 1085 that the order went out for the compilation of the Domesday Book.

The Forest of Dean was a favoured hunting ground for the Norman Kings and Gloucester must have been visited frequently. When King John, William's great-great-grandson, died in 1216, his son was hurriedly crowned at St. Peter's Abbey Gloucester as King Henry III using, it is said, his mother's bracelet for a crown. A century later Henry's grandson, Edward II, was horribly murdered at Berkeley Castle (20 September 1327) and subsequently buried at St. Peter's, his queen, and son Edward III, coming to Gloucester for the state funeral in December 1327.

In the later middle ages, the three Yorkist brothers had quite strong links with the County. Edward IV and his brothers, George Duke of Clarence and Richard Duke of Gloucester, marching along the edge of the Cotswolds overtook Henry VI's queen, Margaret of Anjou, and her son Edward Prince of Wales and defeated them at Tewkesbury (4 May 1471) in which battle Edward Prince of Wales was killed and afterwards buried at Tewkesbury Abbey. Seven years later George Duke of Clarence was executed for treason by drowning in a butt of Malmesey wine, and buried in Tewkesbury Abbey alongside his duchess and not far from his previous adversary, Edward. George's younger brother Richard, later Richard III, caused much of the building at Sudeley Castle but as far as is known rarely if ever stayed there after becoming king. During a progress to Gloucester in August 1483, Richard gave Gloucester its famous charter, the quincentenary of which is to be celebrated in 1983.

Preface

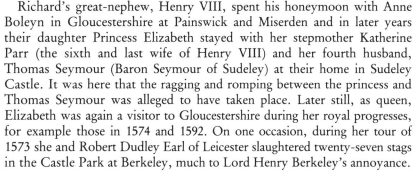

Richard's great-nephew, Henry VIII, spent his honeymoon with Anne Boleyn in Gloucestershire at Painswick and Miserden and in later years their daughter Princess Elizabeth stayed with her stepmother Katherine Parr (the sixth and last wife of Henry VIII) and her fourth husband, Thomas Seymour (Baron Seymour of Sudeley) at their home in Sudeley Castle. It was here that the ragging and romping between the princess and Thomas Seymour was alleged to have taken place. Later still, as queen, Elizabeth was again a visitor to Gloucestershire during her royal progresses, for example those in 1574 and 1592. On one occasion, during her tour of 1573 she and Robert Dudley Earl of Leicester slaughtered twenty-seven stags in the Castle Park at Berkeley, much to Lord Henry Berkeley's annoyance.

With Elizabeth being the last of the Tudors, the succession fell to the line of her executed second cousin, Mary Queen of Scots, in the form of her son, James VI of Scotland. His son Charles I stayed at Painswick and Matson House whilst his forces held Gloucester under seige in 1643. Just as in 1471, when Margaret of Anjou found the city gates closed against her, Charles also found the gates closed and the inhabitants in support of Parliament. After several months the siege was raised by Parliamentary reinforcements from London and Charles retired towards Worcester. It could be argued that this delay outside Gloucester tipped the balance of the Civil War against Charles. During the Restoration Charles II ordered the destruction of the city walls as retribution for the city's defiance of his father.

Over a century later, recognition and prosperity was brought to the new spa of Cheltenham by the arrival of George III and Queen Charlotte to take the waters. While in the County they were entertained by Lord Ducie and one of the relations of the family at Highgrove, Sir George Onesiphorus Paul.

Now, in the twentieth century, seven generations later, it is interesting to see a precedent being set by three members of the Royal family in choosing to make their homes on the beautiful southern Cotswolds, close to Cirencester Park and that favourite annual retreat — Badminton.

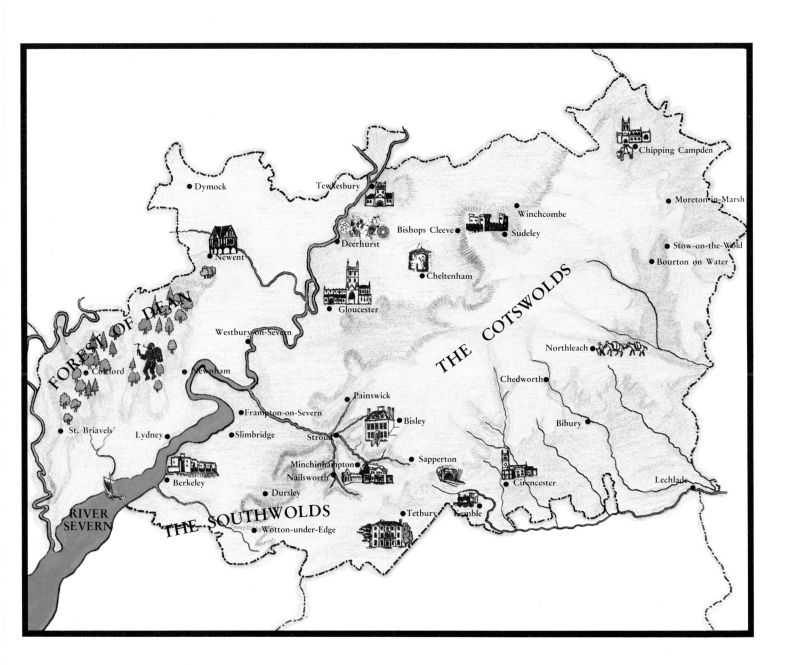

Highgrove

Paul Esqr

F. Slater

Highgrove

John Paul Paul.

Highgrove, Tetbury, the home of the Prince of Wales, was built for John Paul Paul by an unknown architect between 1796 and 1798 on an estate which had belonged to his maternal grandfather Robert Clark.

In _Delineations of Gloucestershire_ (1825 – 7) it was described by J.N. Brewer as:-

> – a substantial and spacious family residence. The design is entirely free from ostentation, although some ornamental particulars are introduced. The principle efforts of the architect have been directed towards the interior, which presents many good apartments, of accurate proportions, well suited to the domestic and hospitable purposes of a family of high respectability. The situation is fine, and excellent views are obtained from the house and various parts of the attached grounds.

Highgrove was severely damaged by fire in 1893 and nearly £6,000 was spent on its restoration in the following year. To quote from _The Buildings of England series, Gloucestershire, Vol. I. The Cotswolds,_ (1970):-

> It is a rectangular three-storey block of five by three bays, with pilasters through the upper floors, cornice, and parapet. A nineteenth-century domestic wing was demolished in 1966 and eighteenth-century fireplaces have been introduced into the house from elsewhere.

Storer's view of Highgrove — *this handsome residence. . .*

The entrance to Highgrove and the lodge of 1798. Tetbury has decided on the replacement of the gates as its wedding present to the Prince

The garden side has bay windows presumably dating from after 1893. Now a large cedar stands near the house and an attractive garden path is lined with golden yews.

There is a spacious entrance hall with well proportioned reception rooms either side.

The lodge of 1798 survives, with a Venetian window, and rusticated gatepiers with fluted friezes; but the town of Tetbury has decided to give the Prince a new pair of gates as a wedding present.

Delineations of Gloucestershire is sometimes called 'Storer's Views' because of the excellent engravings of country houses by J. & H.S. Storer from their own original drawings. They included the lesser country houses, and no-one could pretend that Highgrove was ever in the top flight of country houses in the county; but Brewer, who wrote the text for the Storers, does call it 'this handsome residence', and the engraving is full of charm. In the engraving the front elevation of five bays has a central projecting portico with free-standing columns and a Venetian window above on the first floor. The central three bays break forward, with pilasters through the two upper storeys. The roof is low-pitched behind the cornice and parapet. A carriage and pair are approaching the house along the drive on the left, and in the foreground a gentleman on horseback is talking to a lady and gentleman and a boy with a dog. There is another boy with another dog under a cedar tree, and another gentleman is riding near the house. The park is distinctly flat. Who were these people? The Pauls, observed in the privacy of their home?

The Pauls first came to England as Huguenot immigrants and were established in Gloucestershire in the seventeenth century. They settled in the clothing localities of Woodchester, King's Stanley and Tetbury and, as Dr. E.A.L. Moir says in

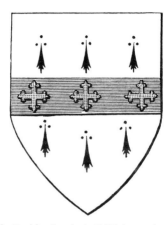

The arms of the Paul family who built Highgrove between 1796 and 1798

The Highgrove estate — *well suited to the domestic and hospitable purposes of a family of high respectability*

Gloucestershire Studies, they were small, moderately prosperous clothiers, distinguished only by their use of the Biblical Christian names Nathaniel, Onesiphorus, Josiah and Obadiah.

The first Paul to settle in Tetbury was Josiah (d. 1744), son of Nathaniel Paul of King's Stanley. He was succeeded by his son John, who died without issue in 1789 and who was succeeded by his nephew Josiah Paul Tippetts, son of his sister Hester, by her marriage with Richard Tippetts of Dursley. In accordance with the will of his maternal uncle, Josiah Paul Tippetts assumed the name of Paul, having married in 1771 Mary, daughter of Robert Clark of Tetbury. Their son John Paul Paul (1772 — 1828) married Mary, only child of Walter Matthews of Clapham, Surrey in 1793.

This lady was an heiress and John Paul Paul must now have been in a position to build a new house on the estate he had inherited through his mother. It is situated in the hamlet of Doughton, and in 1818 Paul purchased the adjoining manor of Doughton for £25,000. In 1807 he was High Sheriff of Wiltshire, having formerly lived at Ashton Keynes which is in that county. When he died in 1828 Highgrove was inherited by his son Walter Matthews Paul, a magistrate for Gloucestershire and Wiltshire, and captain of the Tetbury troop of the Royal Gloucestershire Yeomanry.

Robert Clark Paul (1775 — 1856), John Paul Paul's younger brother, had many interests besides that of clothier. He was for a short time in 1801 a partner in Dyehouse Mill on the Nailsworth stream which forms the boundary between Minchinhampton and Woodchester. It is now owned by Hattersley, Newman Hender Ltd. In 1805 he bought Nag's Head Mill, Cherington, on the Avening stream and his descendants played a leading role in Tetbury as solicitors.

There are several memorials in Tetbury Church to members

of the Paul family, including one to Commander Alfred John Paul, R.N. (1811 – 45), sixth son of Robert Clark Paul, who entered the Royal Navy in 1824, was a midshipman in H.M.S. *Dartmouth* and Flag Lieutenant in H.M.S. *Wellesley* at the taking of Chusan and in the operations against Canton and the subsequent capture of the city of 1841. Another memorial is to Josiah Paul, Lieutenant in the 69th Regiment of Foot, who died in the service of his country at the Helder on the coast of Holland on 28 September 1799 aged twenty years.

The *Victoria County History for Gloucestershire*, volume XI, says that the family interest in the law apparently originated with John Paul (d. 1789), who was the son of Josiah, the first Paul to settle in Tetbury, and who wrote popular legal manuals. Through the descendants of his great nephew Robert Clark Paul the family firm prospered. The principal members of the firm, who held in succession the posts of town clerk and clerk to the feoffees, were J.T. Paul (d. 1875), his son A.H. Paul (d. 1900) and his grandson A.P. Kitcat, who sold the practice in 1935 – Robert Clark Paul's daughter Clara Frances married the Rev. David Kitcat, rector of Lasborough from 1859 to 1906, who lived at Tetbury.

David Kitcat's son Sidney Austyn Paul was born at Tetbury in 1868 and has some claim to fame, for not only was he captain of the Marlborough College cricket XI in 1886, making 204 not out against the Old Marlburians, but he caused the M.C.C. to make an alteration in the laws of cricket. When batting for Marlborough against Rugby he was given out after being caught at cover-point off the bowling of C.W. Bengough, who through an oversight was bowling at the wrong end. The matter was referred to the M.C.C., the law then stating that 'the bowler may not change ends more than twice in the innings, nor bowl more than two overs in

Gloucestershire cricketer, S.A.P. Kitcat (cousin of the Pauls of Highgrove) and W.G. Grace. Between them they added 193 for the ninth wicket against Sussex in 1896 — still a Gloucestershire record

Opposite
Highgrove seen from the garden side with its large cedar and golden yews

Sir George Onesiphorus Paul, famous prison reformer, as depicted in his memorial in Gloucester Cathedral. In his younger days he kept a stable of about a dozen racehorses

succession'. The law was amended in 1889, allowing a bowler 'to change ends as often as he pleases, provided that he does not bowl two consecutive overs in one innings'.

At the early age of thirteen, Kitcat played for Gloucestershire Colts against Gloucestershire in April 1882, but was not tried for the county until 1891. Among his best scores for Gloucestershire were ninety-five not out against Middlesex at Lord's in 1897, which secured him a place in the Gentlemen's side against the Players at the Oval that summer, and seventy-seven not out against Sussex at Bristol in 1896, when he and W.G. Grace (301) added 193 for the ninth wicket, which is still the Gloucestershire record for that wicket.

Walter Matthews Paul, the owner of Highgrove (1828–60), had a sister Mary who married her kinsman Sir John Dean Paul, Bart. in 1835. Sir John Dean Paul was descended from the Rev. Nicholas Paul of Berkeley (d. 1650), who was the father of Nicholas and the Rev. Onesiphorus Paul of Wanborough, Wilts. Nicholas II married Elizabeth, daughter of Thomas Dean of Woodchester and she inherited Southfields Mill, Woodchester, where Frederick Prince of Wales was later entertained. Dean Paul (d. 1794) and Sir Onesiphorus Paul, first baronet, were their sons. The latter's son, Sir George Onesiphorus Paul, second baronet, after an extravagant life in which he kept a stable of about a dozen horses and was a regular supporter of all the local races at Tetbury, Cirencester, Monmouth and Bath, became the famous prison reformer, whose memorial is to be found in Gloucester Cathedral.

When Sir George died in 1820 the baronetcy became extinct, but it was revived in 1821, when Dean Paul's grandson John Dean became the first of the new creation. The latter's first wife was the granddaughter of the eighth Earl of Strathmore, from whom the Queen Mother is descended. Sir John Dean

Paul was the son of John Dean Paul of Salisbury, who married Frances, daughter of Robert Snow of the firm of Snow, Paul and Co., bankers in London.

Walter Matthews Paul's sister Mary, therefore, was the stepmother of the second baronet, Sir John Dean Paul (1802 – 1868), a banker, who to quote the *Dictionary of National Biography*, belonged to the firm of William Strahan, Paul and Robert Makin Bates, which suspended payment in 1855, on which the partners were severally sentenced to fourteen years' penal servitude, as they had fraudulently disposed of their clients' securities.

Sir John was transported to Australia and later the *Madras Times* gave some 'curious information' respecting the 'notorious fraudulent banker, Sir John Dean Paul, Bart., late of Rodborough Manor'. Immediately after he was sentenced to penal servitude, the report stated, Lady Paul realised all the property settled upon her, and proceeded without delay to Sydney, where she purchased a beautiful seat in the suburbs. Her husband having arrived at a penal settlement in another part of Australia, as one of a gang of convicts, she applied to the Government for his services, and was permitted to employ him as her 'assigned servant'. The report added that having thus released him from unpleasant restraint, she placed all the newly-purchased property in his hands, and had since led a quiet life in his company.

In 1860 Walter Matthews Paul sold the combined estate of Doughton Manor and Highgrove to Col. E.J. Strachey and it was acquired in 1864 by William Hamilton Yatman, a barrister, who presented Tetbury Church with a new clock and chimes. The cost of rehanging the bells in the rebuilt tower of Tetbury Church was borne by Yatman in memory of his son Captain Hamilton Yatman, and the view of the spire was kept

Highgrove House — 'substantial and spacious' according to *Delineations of Gloucestershire*

free of trees as he liked to see it from the windows of the house. When Highgrove was severely damaged by fire in 1893 Yatman went to live at Bournemouth, disposing of the estate to Arthur Charles Mitchell (1847 – 1917).

Highgrove was rebuilt by Mitchell, who married, firstly, Laura Harriet (d. 1874), daughter of Sir Michael Hicks-Beach, eighth baronet, and, secondly, Constance Lucy (d. 1945), daughter of John Elwes of Colesborne. He was succeeded by his son Lieutenant-Colonel Francis Arthur Mitchell (1888 – 1955), who commanded the Royal Gloucestershire Hussars and who lived at Doughton Manor while his mother continued to reside at Highgrove.

Lieutenant Colonel Gwyn and the Hon. Mrs. Morgan-Jones were living at Highgrove in the 1960s. In 1974 Highgrove was purchased by Maurice Macmillan, M.P., son of Harold Macmillan, Prime Minister 1957 – 63, and then acquired by the Prince of Wales in 1980.

The Prince of Wales in his own special hunting livery

Tetbury Church from the front door of Highgrove. The gap in the trees was carefully maintained by William Hamilton Yatman in order to ensure that he could see the spire

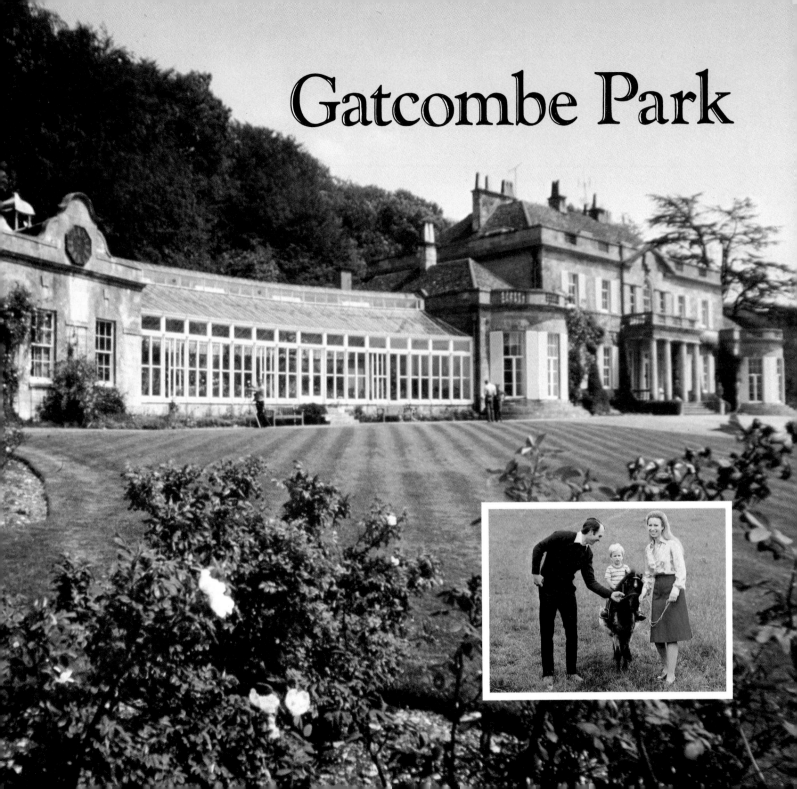

Gatcombe Park

Gatcombe Park

George Basevi, architect of the wings added to Gatcombe around 1820, and cousin of Benjamin Disraeli; from a bust in the Fitzwilliam Museum, which he also designed.

Gatcombe Park, the home of Princess Anne and Captain Mark Phillips, is adjacent to the Avening stream, which marks the boundary between the parishes of Avening and Minchinhampton, both of which manors were granted to Andrew, first Baron Windsor, by Henry VIII in exchange for the Manor of Stanwell, Middlesex (Windsoredge, Nailsworth, derives its name from him).

In 1651 Samuel Sheppard purchased the two manors from the trustees of Lord Windsor. The manor house at Minchinhampton was adjacent to the Church on the site of the present school, but, hemmed in by both town and common, its park no doubt was inadequate to the dignity which the Sheppard family were to attain. Samuel Sheppard III was High Sheriff of Gloucestershire in 1730 and his son Edward, on coming into possession of the property, built a new house at Gatcombe, in a beautiful situation about a mile from Minchinhampton, 1771–4.

This part of the parish is rich in remains of neolithic man. There is a very fine monolith, known as the 'Long Stone', on the north side of the main road within a short distance from Gatcombe Lodge entrance. Tradition says superstitious mothers were in the habit of passing ricketty children through a hole in the stone with the idea that they would by such means become strong. To the east lies the Devil's Churchyard, now part of the Gatcombe estate. There is a local tradition

that a stone circle once stood here and that the stones were moved to The Lammas, Minchinhampton, because unholy rites had been performed on the site. The story is told that it was intended to build a church here; but the building done during the day was pushed down by the Devil during the night, until a new site was chosen and the church built at Minchinhampton.

Gatcombe was described by the historian, Thomas Fosbroke, as 'a fine mansion with a very good front elevation. The plaster work inside the house is in the Adam style, and all the details are extremely well carried out.'

Francis Franklin of Chalford was the mason responsible and possibly the designer. In *c.*1820, after the house had been bought by David Ricardo M.P., the political economist, wings were added by George Basevi, the distinguished architect of the Fitzwilliam Museum at Cambridge. Gatcombe presents an unaltered appearance as even the conservatory was there by 1829. The central block is faced in ashlar, with two storeys and a basement and crowned with a moulded cornice and balustraded parapet. The centre breaks forward with an open pediment above a Venetian window opening on to a balustraded balcony above the porch which has four Doric columns. Either side are one-storey bowed wings. The entrance hall gives on to the main staircase which is partly screened from it by a pair of tall Doric columns. The east side contains the dining room, and the library is beyond, in the single-storeyed wing. The west side has two drawing rooms, with the conservatory beyond. The principal rooms have carved marble chimney pieces.

The stables are built round a polygonal yard with an embattled wall facing the buildings. The grounds are splendidly landscaped, and very pretty.

The 'Long Stone' opposite the entrance to Gatcombe Park. Superstition held that it had power to cure rickets

The stable block built round its polygonal yard

Captain Mark Phillips at Gatcombe

Gatcombe was among the properties featured in *Delineations of Gloucestershire* and described by J.N. Brewer. Gatcombe, he wrote,

– is placed on the ascent of a narrow valley, bounded by high beech wood, with intermingled oak and ash, on one side, whilst the rising ground, in an opposite direction, is decorated with clumps and other efforts of the landscape gardener. The house looks down on a spacious and fine lawn, which terminates in waters, expanded by the hand or art to an ornamental breadth of space. The present elegant house is a well-proportioned and spacious mansion, handsome on the exterior and internally well designed and

Storer's view of Gatcombe — *a well proportioned and spacious mansion*

Interior of the conservatory at Gatcombe

arranged. The chief portico of entrance is highly ornamental to the fabric, and the fine and very extensive conservatory, which adjoins one end of the house and runs in a line with the principal front, is chastely planned and delicately executed.

Edward Sheppard, the builder of Gatcombe, who married Sarah, daughter of Charles Cox of Kemble Park, a family which had also had connections with Nether Lypiatt Manor, died in 1803 aged seventy-eight by which time his new property was already mortgaged. His only son Philip (1766–1838) was the last owner of the estates. He was described by A.T. Playne in his history of Avening and Minchinhampton, as having been an easy-going, good-natured man, very extravagant, and with a great taste for sport and expensive amusements. He raised a troop of Yeomanry in 1795, the equipment and maintenance of which cost him a lot of money. He also kept a pack of hounds at Gatcombe, which were not looked upon with much favour by his father, if we may judge from an entry in a pocket-book of 1790:

> Phil talked of giving up ye hounds; I hope he may continue in ye resolution.

There is, also, in the same pocket-book an account of a great run which Phil had with his hounds from Calcot Barn.

All this now, of course, is Beaufort country. Sheppard was hunting his hounds when the fifth Duke (Master 1786–1803) was increasingly changing his preference from stag to fox hunting.

On his accession to the estate, Philip Sheppard continued his career of extravagance and endeavoured to stave off ruin by mortgages and disposing of parts of his inheritance. Long into the night he and his steward Baldwin would hold consul-

The lodge at the entrance to Gatcombe Park

tations to devise ways and means of tiding over the more pressing difficulties; but the crash came in 1812 and Sheppard escaped to Dunquerque in France, out of reach of his creditors. He eventually died in London in 1838 in very reduced circumstances, leaving two sons Edward and Philip Charles.

William Playne of nearby Longfords acquired the manor of Avening, and David Ricardo, the eminent political economist who had made a fortune on the London Stock Exchange, bought the manor of Minchinhampton and Gatcombe Park. The latter was the son of a Dutch Jew who had settled in England.

In 1823 Ricardo died, being succeeded by his son David, and three years later William Cobbett made one of his *Rural Rides* from Malmesbury to Stroud via Tetbury and Avening. He was on the edge of the high land, looking down upon the village of Avening, he recorded,

. . . a beautiful park, and . . . one of the finest, most magnificent woods. . .

– seeing, just close to it, a large fine mansion-house, a beautiful park, and, making part of the park, one of the finest, most magnificent woods (of 200 acres, I dare say) lying facing me, going from a valley up a gently-rising hill. While I was sitting on my horse, admiring this spot, a man came along with some tools in his hand, as if he were going somewhere to work as a plumber. 'Whose beautiful place is that?' said I. 'One "Squire Ricardo, I think they call him". You might have knocked me down with a feather.' . . .

Cobbett called in at the Cross Inn, Avening, and was told that Gatcombe had belonged to a Mr. Sheppard and to his fathers before him. 'I asked', Cobbett subsequently wrote, 'where this Sheppard was now. A tradesman-looking man told me that he did not know where he was; but that he had heard he

David Ricardo, eminent political economist or, according to Cobbett, *a boroughmonger, of all God's creatures, the basest*

was living somewhere near Bath! Thus they go! Thus they are squeezed out of existence.' Ricardo, he considered, was a 'boroughmonger', of all God's creatures, the basest.

Cobbett, who held radical views, would have known that Ricardo once represented in Parliament the twelve electors of the Irish rotten borough of Portarlington. His son David (1803 – 64) also entered Parliament for a short time, he and W.H. Hyett of Painswick being the first representatives for the new borough of Stroud in 1832.

David Ricardo II was a great benefactor to the manor of Minchinhampton. He built Amberley Church in 1836 and started a school in its basement. The cost of Brimscombe Church, which was begun in 1840, was largely borne by him and he also established a school there, and contributed £2,000 towards the restoration of Minchinhampton Church in 1842. He was also chairman of the Stroud Board of Guardians until 1856. He was succeeded by his son Henry David (1833 – 73), after whose death trustees held the manor until the coming of age of his son Henry George (1860 – 1940).

Henry George Ricardo was educated at Winchester and the Royal Military Academy, Woolwich, and duly commissioned in the Royal Artillery. He retired about 1897. With the outbreak of the Great War in August 1914, it was reported that in Stroud

– there were animated scenes in the yard of the Midland Railway Company, where horses were being brought in from all directions for inspection by the buying officers. About thirty mounts were purchased for the Ninth Lancers by Major Ricardo, and about fifty for the Yeomanry.

Returning to the army, Ricardo found himself in France, where in June 1916 he was mentioned in despatches and in

Gatcombe in its setting at the head of a narrow valley leading down to the Avening Stream

Colonel Henry George Ricardo (second from right), photographed with his three brothers, Rear Admiral Arthur David Ricardo, Captain William Cowley Ricardo and Brigadier General Ambrose St. Quintin Ricardo, all of them aged over fifty and serving in the First World War

January 1917 awarded the Distinguished Service Order. During the war he was photographed with his three brothers, all over fifty years of age – Rear Admiral Arthur David Ricardo, R.N., Captain William Cowley Ricardo of the Canadian Army and Brigadier General Ambrose St. Quintin Ricardo, C.M.G., D.S.O. – by which time Henry George Ricardo had been promoted Lieutenant-Colonel.

Both before and after the war Colonel Ricardo became immersed in public life. He was chairman of the Nailsworth bench of magistrates, for twelve years a county councillor, and for twenty-four president of the Mid-Gloucestershire Conservative Association. At Minchinhampton he was a churchwarden and a parish councillor.

By 1913 he had sold his rights in Minchinhampton Common to the National Trust after increased quarrying had caused alarm. As the second World War approached he found the financial burden of the upkeep of Gatcombe becoming increasingly onerous. Gloucester Lunatic Asylum made an offer of £22,500 for its purchase for the rehousing of patients. However, a neighbour and a former brother-officer, Lord Lee of Fareham, who lived at Old Quarries, Avening, was also interested and, with the support of his great friend, Samuel Courtauld, the property changed hands. Lord Lee is best remembered for his gift of Chequers to the nation as a residence for the Prime Minister and for the storage during the war of some 230 pictures from the National Gallery in his private gallery at Old Quarries.

Gatcombe came under the Courtauld aegis and when Samuel died in 1947 he was succeeded by his son-in-law R.A. Butler, the politician, the farm continuing to be run by a manager. In 1976 Gatcombe became the home of Princess Anne and Captain Mark Phillips.

Nether Lypiatt Manor

ower Lykiatt.
Sept 1895

Nether Lypiatt Manor

Nether Lypiatt Manor, from the north-east and the south, prior to restoration. Note the absence of the dormer windows

Nether Lypiatt Manor, or Lower Lypiatt Hall or the Haunted House, as it has been called at various times, is now the home of Prince and Princess Michael of Kent. From the thirteenth century the manor was the property of the Ream or Freame family and the last direct male was Thomas Freame (d. 1664). He left three heiresses, one of whom, Ann (baptised 1635), married Thomas Chamberlayne of Wanborough, Wilts. Their daughter Catherine married Charles Coxe and she brought to him the manor of Nether Lypiatt. A member of a Rodmarton family, of which place he was subsequently Lord of the Manor, Charles Coxe had a distinguished career as puisne judge of sessions for Brecknock, Glamorgan and Radnor 1702 – 4 and Chief Justice there 1704 – 14. He was M.P. for Cirencester 1693 – 1705 and 1708 – 13 and for Gloucester 1713 – 22.

Judge Coxe entirely rebuilt the mansion at Nether Lypiatt. Miss Mary Rudd in her *Historical Records of Bisley* says the house is built of oolite stone said to be quarried in Bisley, and consists of a barrel vaulted cellar, a basement floor with entrances from north and south, with two storeys of the chief rooms and an attic with a single-span hipped roof, which had two dormer windows on every side until 1848, when the house was practically re-roofed and they were removed. Recent restorations have replaced them. The date 1717, which is that of completion of the house, is to be seen on the rainwater heads of lead, with the Coxe crest, a crowing cock.

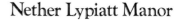

Nether Lypiatt Manor

The forecourt and the road from Brimscombe were separated by ornate gates. It was along this road that Charles I had travelled in the Civil War to undertake the siege of Gloucester. The occasion is recorded in Paul Hawkins Fisher's *Notes and Recollections of Stroud*. The army on 8 August 1643, he wrote,

> – marched from Bristol to Tetbury, a distance of twenty miles; where his Majesty dined, and then proceeded to Cirencester to Sir William Master's 'to supper and bed'. On the next day, the army proceeded to Hampton Road (as Minchinhampton was sometimes called because there the great high roads from Bath to Gloucester, and from Cirencester to the passage of the Severn at Newnham, met and crossed each other) and descended into the Stroud valley at Brimscombe. Here they crossed the river Froom; and, ascending the steep south side of Stroud hill by way of Quar-house, passed directly in front of Lypiatt Hall.

There is a legend that Judge Coxe sentenced to death a smith for murder but pardoned him on condition that he made the gates for his rebuilt house. However, as soon as the gates were completed, the Judge retracted the reprieve, which has given rise to the supposed haunting of the property, both inside and outside the house.

There appears to be absolutely no foundation whatever for this story. Miss Rudd, says that the gates were thought to be the work of Warren of Cambridge, a well-known artificer who made gates at that period, and they could not in any case be the work of a simple local blacksmith. Mr. John Stanton, whose father once owned the property, confirms that the original gates were repaired by Messrs. Chew of Stroud. The screen of stone piers, linked by wrought iron grilles, and with the very fine wrought iron gates, divides the inner from the

The wrought iron gates at Nether Lypiatt, thought to be the work of Warren of Cambridge, and at the root of the story of the supposed haunting

An early photograph of Nether Lypiatt Manor — the perfect grand house in miniature

Nearly all the rooms at Nether Lypiatt have stone bolection-moulded chimney-pieces, but that in the hall is of finely carved white and grey limestone

. . . no house could compose so beautifully for a glass transparency. . .

outer courtyard. It is one of the many remarkable features of the house for which it is listed Grade I. A recent owner sought to close this clairvoyee by building another wall in front. The local authority's objection was upheld by the Department of the Environment, and the wall had to be removed.

Nether Lypiatt Manor is the perfect grand house in miniature. Sir Sacheverell Sitwell has written:

> – no house could compose so beautifully for a glass transparency, with wrought iron gates in front flanked by a pair of little formal pavilions, and with an interior where music will forever linger, for it was the home of Violet Gordon Woodhouse.

Mrs. Woodhouse was a well-known player of the clavichord and harpsichord. Her husband bought the house in 1923, and Lord Barrington, who lived with them, made the garden exceedingly beautiful. The combination of her music and the beauty of the place made a lasting impression on everyone privileged to visit her.

Architecturally the house is of great importance as the elevations of the main building are clearly derived from those at Coleshill (about fifty years earlier and now demolished). The large central chimney stack is intended to take the place of the belvedere or lantern in larger houses such as Coleshill, which Judge Coxe must often have passed on his way to London. The house is only forty-six feet square, but it has a modest English version of the *piano nobile*. Internally the plan is ingenious. All the features of the principal rooms survived when the *Buildings of England* volume on The Cotswolds was published in 1970, though the attic floor had been reconstructed by P. Morley Horder. The principal staircase starts as a dog-leg stair, but by means of off-sets in the walls it widens

gradually until at the top it is of open-well form. The porch has two detached fluted Ionic columns supporting a segmental pediment approached up a flight of thirteen steps.

Wings stand corner to corner with the house to the N.W. (added by P. Morley Horder in 1923), S.W., and S.E. All the buildings are faced in Cotswold ashlar of admirable quality and roofed with Cotswold stone slates.

P.H. Fisher records the erection in Lower Lypiatt Wood by Judge Coxe of an obelisk in memory of a favourite horse which died in 1721. The inscription is:-

> *My name was Wag, that rolled the green,*
> *The oldest horse that ever was seen.*
> *My years — they numbered forty-two —*
> *I served my master just and true.*

Judge Coxe died in 1729 and was buried at Rodmarton. He left to his son John (1695–1783), a barrister who was M.P. for Cirencester 1749–54, his mansion at Lypiatt and to his grandson Charles his manors of Rodmarton, Tarlton and Hayley and lands in Sapperton, Oddington, Avening, Stroud and Bisley. In time the grandson also inherited Nether Lypiatt.

In 1749 Charles Coxe II married Elizabeth, a daughter and eventual co-heir of Sir Robert Westley, lord mayor of London in 1743. Charles Westley Coxe of Kemble House, their only son, inherited his father's manors including Nether Lypiatt and from his mother the manors of Poole Keynes. He was M.P. for North Wiltshire. In 1789 he married Ann, daughter of Robert Gordon of Auchendolly, and died in 1806. Charles Westley Coxe's only daughter and heir Elizabeth Ann succeeded to all her father's manors and property and in 1809 she married her cousin Robert Gordon (d. 1864) of Auchendolly and of Lewiston House, Dorset.

The obelisk in memory of Wag —
the oldest horse that ever was seen

Nether Lypiatt Manor

Kemble was on the planned route of the railway line from Swindon to Cheltenham and in 1836 Gordon was paid £7,500 as 'compensation for damage to be sustained'. He also demanded that the railway should be in a covered way where it passed Kemble House. This explains the tunnel, 415 yards long, which has existed to this day. He also stipulated that there should be no public station on the estate and it was not until 1879, when a director of the Great Western, with about twenty other passengers, finding himself herded in a small shed in bitter cold, opened negotiations with Gordon's only daughter and heir Anna that one was built. She made a stipulation that there should be no refreshment room for the sale of alcohol.

In the Bisley Tithe Terrier of 1841 Mrs. Ann Gordon, mother of Anna, is shown as the owner of Lower Lypiatt House and Robert Ridler as her tenant. Mrs. Gordon was the occupier of Berrimans and she also owned Monument and Mackhouse Woods and the beer house which became known as the Forester's.

Anna Gordon (1809—84) left her manors, apart from Nether Lypiatt, to Michael Biddulph of Ledbury, a great friend of her father (in accordance with his wishes). About 1880 she gave Nether Lypiatt to a distant cousin, Philip Charles Sheppard, son of Philip Sheppard of Gatcombe, thereby carrying out the provision of her grandmother's will. She also presented to the School of Art, Gloucester, three fine pieces of tapestry of late seventeenth-century work, which had adorned the drawing room.

Nether Lypiatt Manor itself was tenanted for many years by farmers. William Gardner, of Scottish descent, died in 1812 and was buried in Bisley. In 1812 it was leased to George Ridler (d. 1837) and his great great great granddaughter Mrs.

The lawn mower, invented by Edwin Budding at Thrupp in 1830, similar to that illustrated in Ransome and May's catalogue of 1851, with Nether Lypiatt in the background

Nether Lypiatt Manor

Margery Ridler Dutton Hawkes adds the information that two of his children, his son Robert and daughter Jane, inherited the lease of Nether Lypiatt Manor. Robert died in 1845 aged thirty-five and his sister, who married Charles Ractliffe, died in 1876 at the Manor. Ractliffe's daughter Elizabeth Jane married William Thomas Wallis, after whose death his son Charles Pearson Wallis carried on the farming until 1915, when the connected tenancy was broken.

The property, being in the hands of mortgagees, was sold to Arthur William Stanton before the First World War. The son of Walter John Stanton, a woollen cloth manufacturer, who was M.P. for Stroud, February to May 1874, when he was unseated on petiton, and 1880 – 5, A.W. Stanton (1875 – 1944) himself contested several parliamentary elections unsuccessfully. He never lived at Nether Lypiatt because he had inherited other properties in the Stroud district. He, however, employed Morley Horder, an architect, to prepare plans for its occupation and some of the more urgent repairs, including the gates, were carried out. Nether Lypiatt was acquired by Corbett W. Woodhall, a restorer of many ancient houses, and with the assistance of Morley Horder a complete and most satisfactory restoration was effected.

In 1923 Woodhall sold the property to Mr. and Mrs. Gordon Woodhouse, and its subsequent owners were her nephew, John Gwynne, Frederick Nettlefold, Major L.V.L.W. Barrington and Simon Boyle, before being bought by Prince and Princess Michael of Kent in 1980.

eep shearing in front of Nether Lypiatt before the First World ar. The Manor was tenanted for many years by farmers

e south side of Nether Lypiatt Manor, showing the garden and restored dormer windows

Acknowledgements

Alan Sutton Publishing Limited
17a Brunswick Road
Gloucester GL1 1HG

Produced in association with:

Severnprint Limited
Ashville Industrial Estate
Gloucester

British Library Cataloguing in Publication Data

Sanders, Geoffrey
  Royal homes in Gloucestershire.
  1. Country homes - England - Gloucestershire -
  History   2. Great Britain - Kings and rulers
  I. Title   II. Verey, David
  942.4'1   DA690.G5

  ISBN 0-904387-89-5

Basic text by Geoffrey Sanders with architectural notes by David Verey. Designed by Chris Norman. Picture research by Peter Clifford.

Picture credits:

Aerofilms Ltd.: *aerial view of Highgrove estate.* Camera Press Ltd.: *black and white view of Highgrove; conservatory and stable block at Gatcombe; black and white and colour views of Gatcombe; Royal portraits.* Jack Farley: *Sir George Onesiphorus Paul.* Fitzwilliam Museum, Cambridge: *George Basevi.* S.J. Gardiner: *north-east and south fronts of Nether Lypiatt prior to restoration.* Gloucestershire Record Office: *John Paul Paul signature.* Gloucestershire County Library: *Storer engravings; nineteenth-century drawings of Highgrove, Gatcombe and Nether Lypiatt; Judge Coxe signature.* Peter Harding: *colour views of Highgrove House; Prince Charles on horseback; Tetbury Church.* National Monuments Record, Crown Copyright: *black and white views of Nether Lypiatt showing gates, chimneypiece and south front with garden.* National Portrait Gallery Archives: *David Ricardo.* Geoffrey Sanders: *S.A.P. Kitcat; Ricardo brothers.* R. Sollars: *Edwin Budding's lawnmower.* Sunday Times: *Captain Mark Phillips at Gatcombe.* Peter Turner: *colour views of Nether Lypiatt.* Illustrations: Chris Norman; Martin Latham; Davina Wynne-Jones, Gryffon Press.

Photosetting and origination by Alan Sutton Publishing Limited. Set Stempel Garamond 12/14. Printed in Great Britain by Severnprint Limited.